M000311069

# Out Of Doors

*Poems From A Pacific Northwest Forest*

DAVID GRETCH

Ordering Information:

For orders and inquiries, please contact:
1-888-375-9818
www.toplinkpublishing.com
bookorder@toplinkpublishing.com


Printed in the United States of America

# The Rock

the rock

aware
hurdling
thru space

condensed
perfectly
content

# Chief

ancient mountain
proud and strong
listen closely
timeless song

silken skin of
fragrant trees
home for all
birds and bees
mammals critters
all of these
playing dearly
gentle breeze

face of granite
knowing why
lie beneath
holy sky
soft caress
you make me cry

# Pump House

feel the ground
hear old pump house sound
look around
forest beauty greens abound

breathe the sky
touch cool breeze passing by
natural high
tender moments never die

# Dirt Floor

beginning in between
birth and deaths
so many breaths
dying moments
bright beginnings
where am I going?

lottery winnings
build a cabin
without a door
rustic decor
grow some grassroots
dirt floor

no deposit
no return
no concern
empty center
fill with life
moments dying
new beginnings
where I'm going

dirt floor

# Nature's Breath

nature's breath,
      softest breeze,
            feigning stillness
                  with young trees

just a scent
i am aware
she waits for me...
            to breathe her air

dizzy then
      i do become
            knowing that
               it's not from rum

intoxication by
            nature...
                  sets me free...

# Forest Wren

forest wren
lovely melody
in a log again
evaporating clarity

                          tenderly hiding

peeps...

sweetly sung...
         from that clump
              of well knit moss
                  sweetly veiling
peeps...

              i hear him now,
          over there
       in that fern
i think he hides...

      where are you now,
forest boss?
      can't find you,
          at a loss...

smell
    sweet breeze

off leaves a glisten

                take it in,
                 softly listen...
         smell love forest
      dark and wet
exhale now
      let go regret

forest moment transcend time
        traveling chill down my spine
when it's over, what will stay?
       silent memory peaceful day

lay me down on silken rug
      close my eyes, cozy snug
at this moment i am free
      forest wren sing to me

# Forest Cave

ride subliminal love wave
hangout in forest cave
surrender to chocolate crave

sip damp and fragrant forest air
feel within an ancient lair
life sacred everywhere

# Forest Stroll

forest stroll
nature watching
        nature sees
           crispy breeze
                pleasant scent of
                    cedar trees

sweetest birds
      delicious
         varieties of sound
              rapid flight
           weaving
                 darting
                 around

chipmunk
    join
     joyous
       jubilation
         laughing voice
           good vibration

soothing sun
      bumble bees in a time freeze
             killing hours with flowers
squirrel
   plays
     with
      trees

forest stroll,
     timeless flight
         away from pain,
            into dance
           natures best
      could not have come
          by circumstance

# The Road Home

30 days solid rain
smell damp earth
solar entrance once again
bring rebirth

cool damp mist softly rise
sights unknown
illuminate for my eyes
the road home

# Like a Tree

breathing
from your thoughts
from your head
from your bed
about your dread
of being dead
when instead
you should breathe
from your soul
your quiet below
peace heart know
proper mind show
thoughts become

breathe on

like a fawn
or a swan
mother dawn
slightly yawn
dwelling long
peaceful song

breathe on

like a tree
happily
n free
listening
winged brother
turning air into song
breathe along
belong

# Slow Dancing

slow
  dancing
        friends
crispy
  brown
      leaves
trunk
  slowly
        moves
just
  a
      couple
                  degrees

hang
  onto
      branches
                slow
          spin
  around
mutual
  embrace
roots
on
g
r
o
u
n
d
.

dancing trees
          dance till dawn

# Circles

circles within circles

pause to view Master Plan
beyond intelligence of man

life within lives
lives within life
mystery directs
wisdom reflects

circles connected to circles

spin a family pure delight
young and old sleep at night
each unique yet all are one
never finished always done

johnys walking just turned two
loves to try to tie his shoe
suzies fine she just turned four
likes to lock the bathroom door

bridges joining circles

new experiences every day
sprinkle in some miracles
joyous years and conquered fears
connected through smiles and tears

suzies home from soccer late
feed her quick she has a date
johny asked to drive your car
said he wont go very far

circles within circles

unite all pain and pleasure
create a family treasure

grandkids coming bake a pie
off to town ice cream to buy
flapjack eggs next morn will do
honey life's so good with you

building circles
bridging miracles

# Spring Dream

pacific
northwest
mountain
huckleberry
bush

soaked in sun

buds and flowers
springtime berries
dessert story

warm huckleberry cobbler with vanilla ice cream

# Thunderstorm

like a thunderstorm
sets apart a spring day warm
leaves an imprint
thunder sky
dark shutter rumble

so this mood of discontent
as if Heaven sent
replies to higher states
and negates
their curious perfection

like so close lightening bolt
predicts a supersonic jolt
thunder boom
shakes the room
why suffer variety

magnificent deathly quiet
not a single drop of rain
distant angry rumble
dark brew
starts humble

sly swirling wind around
lightening find safe ground
what a way to end
must say
a warm spring day

# Wind Storm

inevitably stormy night
treacherous invite
go for a walk
feel peril stalk
paying penance
crashing entrance
autumn explosion greatness
rage of dynamite
hundred and fifty foot firs
been here two hundred years
leaning and rocking
clicking and knocking
against onslaught of
atmospheric ferocity
whipping immensity
swirls and gusts
blazing yellow leaves
from autumns maple
screaming through the air
at bullet speed
vision blurring projectiles
look up, sky roars
giants bending backs bowed
imagination, my racing heart
trees uproot, branches breaking
hardwood tons crashing down
right around
this place
i stand
in fear

# From Within

viewed from within
trees with
staggering beauty
stunning curves
swarming green
moss on fire
and frame
black aglow

view from within
womb and child
one love
flowing
between two lives
tender emotions
travel in waves
very slow

view from within
scent of coal
all I know
summarized
charcoal glow
mind parked
mystified
silent show

# Tree Ice

delicate tree ice
decorated sleeping hand
holding wispy breeze

# Secret Place

water
life
fall
aqueous
roaring moments
descending hillside
from yesterday
impact conscience
understanding
wash away doubt
hydrate hope

escape
pain
regret
suffering
secret place
behind mind
nurtured silence
soothing darkness
tranquility of night
emotional warmth
behind mind
below light
holiness
all engraved
peaceful sight

# Salmonberry Trout

There's this recipe for life
out in Nature;
it's simple.
Wander over salted waters
to mountains named Olympics;
drive a road,
load a pack,
walk a mountain trail
to simple wooded lake,
pristine water,
shaded from distress,
mostly cedar, fir and pine.
Pitch a tent, build a
fire,
take a walk,
follow black bear
to salmonberry bush,
make a wish.
Pick with prayer,
a capful
of sweetly succulent
red yellow orange mountain
salmonberries.
Dig a worm, bait a hook,
catch a rainbow trout or two,
stuff with berries,
wrap in foil,
roast on fire coals.
Spirit of pure lake
tastes divine.

# After Thought

leave thought
ignore impulse
brush aside feelings of
what i ain't got
abandon belonging to
man made reality
shake away cobweb
wave away cloud
make haste
shiver away all learned and acquired taste

melt among primal pool
with every motion
recover emotion
precious jewel
refocus
tune in

cool breath on the soft breeze as it undulates through the
effervescent trees

CPSIA information can be obtained
at www.ICGtesting.com
Printed in the USA
LVHW071210150419
614196LV00003B/15/P